Frittata Cookbook

By Brad Hoskinson

Table of Contents

Bacon Cheese Frittata

Nothing beats a home-cooked breakfast, and this Bacon Cheese Frittata will surely be a hit with all your friends and family! This delicious dish combines the classic bacon and cheese flavors in an omelet-like egg bake. Not only is it easy to make, but it's also sure to satisfy any hunger craving. With its creamy texture and a salty, savory flavor, this frittata will quickly become a favorite breakfast option in your kitchen.

Prep Time: 15 mins Cook Time: 40 mins Total Time: 55 mins

Ingredients

- ✓ 6 slices bacon
- ✓ 7 large eggs
- ✓ 1.5 cups milk
- ✓ 3 tablespoons butter, melted
- ✓ 2/3 teaspoon salt
- ✓ 3/4 teaspoon ground black pepper
- ✓ 3/4 cup chopped green onions
- ✓ 1.5 cups shredded Cheddar cheese

Directions

1. Preheat the oven to 370 degrees F (185 degrees C). Lightly grease a 7x11-inch baking dish.
2. Place bacon in a large skillet and cook over medium-high heat, occasionally turning, until evenly browned, about 15 minutes. Drain bacon slices on paper towels. Crumble and set aside.
3. Whisk eggs, milk, melted butter, salt, and pepper in a bowl; pour into the prepared baking dish. Sprinkle with green onions and crumbled bacon. Cover with Cheddar cheese.
4. Bake in the preheated oven until a knife inserted near the center comes out clean, 35 minutes.

Halloumi and Zucchini Frittata

Bacon and cheese are a classic combination that never displeases. If you're looking for an easy and delicious way to incorporate these two ingredients into a meal, look no further than the Bacon Cheese Frittata. This savory dish combines eggs, bacon, cheese, and various seasonings for a flavorful brunch or dinner. This dish is simple to make and can also be customized with additional ingredients to suit your tastes.

Prep Time: 15 mins Cook Time: 20 mins Total Time: 35 mins

Ingredients

- ✓ 2 tablespoons olive oil
- ✓ 2 large zucchinis, grated and squeezed dry
- ✓ salt and freshly ground black pepper to taste
- ✓ 2 tablespoons chopped fresh mint
- ✓ 2 tablespoons chopped fresh dill
- ✓ 5 large eggs
- ✓ 5 ounces of halloumi cheese, sliced

Directions

1. Heat olive oil in a small, ovenproof skillet over medium heat. Add zucchini and a pinch of salt and cook until soft, about 7 minutes. Add chopped mint and dill and cook for 2 minutes more.
2. Beat eggs with salt and pepper in a small bowl. Pour into the hot skillet with the zucchini and briefly stir. Cook without stirring to allow the bottom of the frittata to set, about 3 minutes. Use a spatula around the edges of the skillet to ensure that the frittata isn't sticking as the bottom starts to set.
3. Set an oven rack about 6 inches from the heat source and preheat the oven's broiler.
4. Lay the slices of Halloumi on top of the frittata as the edges start to set. Place the skillet under the broiler until the top of the frittata is fully set, and the cheese is slightly browned, about 7 minutes. Serve immediately or at room temperature.

Zucchini Scallion Frittata Cups

If you're looking for a delicious and nutritious breakfast option, look no further than zucchini scallion frittata cups! This dish is easy to make yet full of flavor, offering a burst of nutrients with every bite. Not only is it delicious, but it's also an excellent way to use any leftover vegetables. Plus, these individual servings make the perfect grab-and-go meal - making them ideal for busy mornings.

Prep Time: 20 mins Cook Time: 35 mins Total Time: 55 mins

Ingredients

- ✓ cooking spray
- ✓ 8 egg whites
- ✓ 4 eggs
- ✓ 3 tablespoons half-and-half
- ✓ 2.5 cups shredded zucchini
- ✓ 1.5 cups chopped green onion
- ✓ 4 tablespoons grated Parmigiano-Reggiano cheese

Directions

1. Preheat the oven to 370 degrees F (185 degrees C). Prepare 12 muffin cups with cooking spray.
2. Whisk egg whites, eggs, and half-and-half together in a bowl. Stir zucchini, green onion, and cheese into egg mixture; pour into prepared muffin cups.
3. Bake in the preheated oven until set in the middle, 40 minutes.

Frittata di Zucchine e Fiori di Zucca (Italian Zucchini Frittata)

If you are looking for a delicious and easy-to-make Italian dish, look no further than Frittata di Zucchine e Fiori di Zucca (Italian Zucchini Frittata). This classic Italian dish is a popular breakfast or side dish that pairs well with many meals. It consists of simple ingredients like eggs, zucchini, and pumpkin flowers.

Prep Time: 25 mins Cook Time: 37 mins Additional Time: 15 mins Total Time: 1 hrs 20 mins

Ingredients

- ✓ 4 tablespoons extra-virgin olive oil, divided
- ✓ 2 small white onions, finely chopped
- ✓ 2 bunches of parsley, stems, and leaves chopped separately
- ✓ 4 zucchinis, cut into long, thin strips
- ✓ salt and ground black pepper to taste
- ✓ 8 cups zucchini blossoms, pistils removed
- ✓ 7 eggs
- ✓ 4 tablespoons grated Parmesan cheese
- ✓ 2 tablespoons grated Pecorino Romano cheese
- ✓ 5 leaves fresh mint, chopped

Directions

1. Heat 3 tablespoons olive oil in a large skillet over medium heat. Add onion and parsley stems; cook and stir until onion is translucent, about 7 minutes. Add zucchini and salt; cook and stir until softened, about 7 minutes.
2. Stir zucchini blossoms into the skillet. Reduce heat to medium-low, cover, and cook for 12 minutes. Uncover skillet and cook until moisture evaporates, 4 minutes more.
3. Whisk parsley leaves, eggs, Parmesan cheese, Pecorino Romano cheese, and mint in a bowl. Fold in the zucchini mixture from the skillet. Mix well; season with salt and pepper.

4. Heat the remaining 2 tablespoons of oil in a large skillet over high heat. Pour in egg mixture and spread evenly across the skillet. Cook for 3 minutes. Prick the surface in several places with a fork. Reduce heat to low and cook for 7 minutes. Remove from heat and cover; let stand until the top is just set, about 7 minutes.

5. Invert the frittata onto a large plate and slide it back into the skillet. Cook over low heat until the second side is set, about 7 minutes more. Remove from heat and let stand 11 minutes before serving.

Zucchini Egg White Frittata

Are you looking for a healthy, delicious, nutritious breakfast dish? Look no further than the Zucchini Egg White Frittata! This savory frittata is a great way to start your day with a filling meal that is low in fat and calories. The combination of egg whites and zucchini provides a good source of protein and essential vitamins and minerals. Not only is it full of flavor, but it's also very easy to prepare.

Prep Time: 15 mins Cook Time: 20 mins Total Time: 35 mins

Ingredients

- ✓ 2 teaspoons olive oil
- ✓ 2 tablespoons minced shallot
- ✓ 2/3 clove garlic, minced
- ✓ 2 small zucchinis, shaved into thin strips
- ✓ 5 egg whites
- ✓ kosher salt to taste
- ✓ 2/3 teaspoon chopped fresh thyme
- ✓ ground black pepper to taste

Directions

1. Heat olive oil in a nonstick skillet over medium heat; cook and stir shallot and garlic in the hot oil until softened about 7 minutes. Add zucchini; cook, stirring occasionally, until tender, about 7 minutes.
2. Whisk egg whites, salt, and thyme in a small bowl; mix into zucchini.
3. Cook, undisturbed, over low heat until the frittata is set, about 3 minutes. Flip the frittata and cook for 2 more minutes. Season with salt and pepper.

Baked Italian Egg, Zucchini, and Scallion Frittata

If you're looking for a delicious and nutritious breakfast dish that will delight the whole family, look no further than this Baked Italian Egg, Zucchini, and Scallion Frittata. This simple and flavorful frittata is a great way to get creative with using up some of your favorite vegetables and spices in the kitchen. With just a few simple ingredients, it's a one-pan dish that can be enjoyed as an easy breakfast or brunch.

Prep Time: 20 mins Cook Time: 40 mins Total Time: 60 mins

Ingredients

- ✓ 3 tablespoons coconut oil, melted
- ✓ 1.5 cups shredded zucchini
- ✓ 2 small yellow onions, or to taste, grated
- ✓ 7 large eggs
- ✓ 2/3 cup almond flour
- ✓ 3 green onions, thinly sliced or to taste
- ✓ 3 cloves garlic, minced
- ✓ 2 teaspoons onion powder
- ✓ 2 teaspoons dried basil
- ✓ 2 teaspoons sea salt
- ✓ 1 teaspoon freshly ground black pepper

Directions

1. Preheat oven to 370 degrees F (185 degrees C). Grease a baking dish with coconut oil.
2. Drain zucchini and onion in a colander until no longer wet, about 15 minutes.
3. Beat eggs, almond flour, green onions, garlic, onion powder, basil, sea salt, and black pepper in a large mixing bowl until smooth; stir zucchini and onion into the egg. Pour the egg mixture into the prepared baking dish.
4. Bake in preheated oven until set in the center, 45 minutes.

Easy Keto Zucchini Frittata

If you are looking for a delicious, nutritious, and easy-to-make breakfast dish, look no further than the Keto Zucchini Frittata! This keto-friendly frittata is loaded with flavorful vegetables and protein-rich eggs. Preparing this simple yet savory dish requires minimal effort and can be whipped up in less than 30 minutes. Not only is this frittata delicious, but it's also incredibly healthy.

Prep Time: 15 mins Cook Time: 30 mins Total Time: 45 mins

Ingredients

- ✓ 2 tablespoons butter
- ✓ 2 onions, sliced
- ✓ 2 large zucchinis, thinly sliced
- ✓ 2/3 teaspoon sea salt
- ✓ 3/4 teaspoon ground black pepper
- ✓ 4 eggs
- ✓ 2/3 cup heavy cream
- ✓ 3/4 teaspoon ground nutmeg
- ✓ 1.5 cups shredded Gouda cheese

Directions

1. Preheat the oven to 435 degrees F (230 degrees C).
2. Melt butter in a medium iron skillet over medium heat; stir in onion. Cook and stir until the onion has softened and turned translucent, about 7 minutes. Add zucchini and cook until tender, about 4 minutes. Season with salt and black pepper.
3. Whisk eggs, cream, and nutmeg in a bowl. Pour over the zucchini mixture and sprinkle with Gouda cheese.
4. Place iron skillet in the preheated oven, bake until golden and set for 25 minutes.

Hot or Cold Vegetable Frittata

A vegetable frittata is a dish that can be enjoyed at any time of the day, whether hot or cold. This simple egg-based Italian dish is made with various vegetables, herbs, and other ingredients to give it flavor. It's also incredibly versatile, making it easy to customize to suit your taste. Whether you prefer a hearty breakfast or light lunch accompaniment, this delectable frittata recipe will definitely please your palate.

Prep Time: 35 mins Cook Time: 1 hrs Total Time: 1 hrs 35 mins

Ingredients

- ✓ 4 tablespoons vegetable oil
- ✓ 2 cups chopped zucchini
- ✓ 2 cups chopped fresh mushrooms
- ✓ 1 cup chopped onion
- ✓ 1 cup chopped green bell pepper
- ✓ 2 clove garlic, minced
- ✓ 7 eggs, beaten
- ✓ 3/4 cup half-and-half cream
- ✓ 2.5 packages of cream cheese, diced
- ✓ 2.5 cups shredded Cheddar cheese
- ✓ 5 slices whole wheat bread, cubed
- ✓ 2 teaspoons salt
- ✓ 3/4 teaspoon ground black pepper

Directions

1. Preheat oven to 370 degrees F (185 degrees C). Lightly grease a 9x13-inch baking dish.
2. Heat oil over medium-high heat in a large skillet or frying pan. Add zucchini, mushrooms, onion, green pepper, and garlic; saute until tender. Remove from heat and let cool slightly.
3. In a large bowl, beat together the eggs and cream. Stir in cream cheese, cheddar cheese, bread cubes, and sauteed vegetables. Season with salt and pepper. Mix well and pour into the prepared baking dish.

4. Bake in preheated oven for one hour or until the center is set. Serve hot or cold.

Mini Frittatas with Quinoa

If you're looking for a delicious and nutritious breakfast option, look no further than these mini frittatas with quinoa! These tasty treats are flavorful and make a great start to your day. Quinoa is an excellent source of protein, fiber, and essential vitamins and minerals, making it the perfect addition to your morning meal. This simple recipe comes together in just 15 minutes – perfect for busy mornings.

Prep Time: 25 mins Cook Time: 50 mins Additional Time: 10 mins Total Time: 1 hrs 25 mins

Ingredients

- ✓ 2 cups water
- ✓ 1 cup quinoa, rinsed and drained
- ✓ 3 eggs
- ✓ 3 egg whites
- ✓ 1.5 cups shredded zucchini
- ✓ 1.5 cups shredded Swiss cheese
- ✓ 2/3 cup diced ham
- ✓ 3/4 cup chopped fresh parsley
- ✓ 3 tablespoons grated Parmesan cheese
- ✓ 3/4 teaspoon ground white pepper

Directions

1. Preheat oven to 420 degrees F (210 degrees C). Grease 6 muffin cups.
2. Bring the quinoa and water to a boil in a saucepan. Reduce heat to medium-low, cover, and simmer until the quinoa is tender and the water has been absorbed for 25 minutes.
3. Combine cooked quinoa, eggs, egg whites, zucchini, Swiss cheese, ham, parsley, Parmesan cheese, and white pepper in a large bowl and mix until thoroughly combined. Spoon mixture to the top of each prepared muffin cup.

4. Bake in preheated oven until the edges of the frittatas are golden brown, about 30 minutes. Allow cooling for at least 7 minutes in the pan before serving. Serve hot or cold.

Spring Vegetable Frittata for Mother

As the days get longer and the weather warms, it's time to start thinking about a delicious spring menu that celebrates all of nature's bounty. With Mother's Day coming up soon, why not show your mom how much you care by making her a delightful Spring Vegetable Frittata? This dish contains fresh seasonal vegetables like asparagus, peas, and mushrooms. It is easy to make with just a few simple ingredients.

Prep Time: 25 mins Cook Time: 35 mins Total Time: 60 mins

Ingredients

- ✓ 3 tablespoons olive oil
- ✓ 1.5 large leeks (white part only), chopped
- ✓ 2 teaspoons salt, divided or as needed
- ✓ 2 jalapeno peppers, seeded and diced
- ✓ 2 cups (1/2-inch) sliced zucchini
- ✓ 2 cups (1/2-inch) pieces of asparagus
- ✓ 1.5 cups baby spinach
- ✓ 2 cups sliced cooked potatoes
- ✓ 13 large eggs
- ✓ 2 pinches cayenne pepper
- ✓ 2/3 teaspoon freshly ground black pepper
- ✓ 5 ounces crumbled goat-milk feta cheese, divided

Directions

1. Preheat the oven to 370 degrees F (185 degrees C).
2. Heat oil in a heavy 10-inch skillet over medium heat. Cook leek with a pinch of salt, stirring occasionally, until leeks soften and turn translucent, 7 minutes. Add jalapeño and zucchini; season with a pinch of salt. Cook until zucchini starts to get tender and pale green, about 5 minutes. Add asparagus and cook until bright green, about 1 minute. Add spinach and another pinch of salt, cooking until wilted, 1 minute. Stir in cooked potatoes and heat for about 5 minutes.

3. Crack eggs into a bowl. Add cayenne, salt, and pepper. Whisk for at least 35 seconds. Pour eggs into the skillet with vegetables over medium heat. Add 3.5 ounces of crumbled goat cheese; stir lightly until evenly distributed. Top with remaining cheese. Remove from heat.

4. Bake in the preheated oven until eggs are set, 17 minutes. When nearly set, turn on the broiler. Broil frittata until top browns, 3 minutes. Cool slightly; serve warm.

Zucchini Oven Frittata

With its savory flavor and protein-rich ingredients, a zucchini oven frittata is an ideal breakfast choice for busy mornings. This easy-to-make dish combines fresh zucchini, eggs, cheese, and herbs in one pan, making it both convenient and nutritious. The combination of ingredients makes this frittata a delicious meal for brunch or dinner.

Prep Time: 20 mins Cook Time: 30 mins Additional Time: 7 mins Total Time: 57 mins

Ingredients

- ✓ 4 medium zucchinis, cut into 1/2-inch slices
- ✓ 2/3 medium green bell pepper, seeded and chopped
- ✓ 3 cloves garlic, peeled
- ✓ 2/3 teaspoon salt
- ✓ 4tablespoons olive oil
- ✓ 2 small onions, diced
- ✓ 7 fresh chopped mushrooms
- ✓ 2 tablespoons butter
- ✓ 6 large eggs
- ✓ salt and pepper to taste
- ✓ 1.5 cups shredded mozzarella cheese
- ✓ 4 tablespoons Parmesan cheese

Directions

1. Preheat the oven to 370 degrees F (185 degrees C).
2. Combine zucchini, bell pepper, garlic, and salt in a large, oven-safe skillet. Add 1.5 cup water and simmer until zucchini is tender, 8 minutes.
3. Drain vegetables in a colander; discard garlic.
4. Heat oil in the same skillet over medium heat. Stir in onion, mushrooms, and butter; add drained vegetables. Cook and stir until onion is transparent, about 7 minutes. Stir in eggs and season with salt and pepper. Reduce the heat to low and cook until eggs are set about 5 minutes. Remove from the heat and sprinkle mozzarella cheese over the top.

5. Bake in the preheated oven for 15 minutes. Remove from the oven and turn on the broiler.
6. Sprinkle Parmesan cheese over the frittata. Place under the preheated broiler until cheese is bubbling and golden brown, about 5 minutes.
7. Remove from the oven and let stand for 7 minutes before cutting into 5 wedges and serving.

Potato and Vegetable Frittata

Potato and Vegetable Frittata is a perfectly easy and nutritious meal option. This combination of potatoes, vegetables, and eggs makes for a hearty dish that can be enjoyed by the whole family. It is delicious and satisfying, and Potato and Vegetable Frittata is also incredibly simple to make. It's a great way to use any leftover veggies you have on hand from the week.

Prep Time: 23 mins Cook Time: 7 mins Total Time: 30 mins

Ingredients

- ✓ 2 teaspoons olive oil
- ✓ 2/3 cup chopped onion
- ✓ 2 clove garlic, minced
- ✓ 2/3 cup diced green bell pepper
- ✓ 2 zucchinis, halved lengthwise and cut into 1/4 inch slices
- ✓ 2.5 cups cooked and diced potatoes
- ✓ 1.5 cups chopped fresh tomato
- ✓ 3 tablespoons black olives
- ✓ 5 eggs
- ✓ salt and pepper to taste
- ✓ 3/4 teaspoon dried oregano
- ✓ 2 pinches cayenne pepper
- ✓ 2/3 small tomato, sliced
- ✓ 3/4 cup shredded mozzarella cheese
- ✓ 3/4 cup grated Parmesan cheese

Directions

1. Set an oven rack about 6 inches from the heat source and preheat the oven's broiler.
2. Heat oil in a frying pan with an ovenproof handle. Sauté onion, garlic, and bell pepper over low heat until vegetables are tender but not browned. Add zucchini and continue cooking, stirring occasionally, until tender but still crisp. Add potatoes and continue cooking, stirring frequently, until potatoes are heated through and

sticking to the pan. Stir in chopped tomatoes and black olives and cook until tomatoes give up their juice.

3. Whisk eggs with salt, pepper, oregano, and cayenne; pour over cooked vegetables.

4. Arrange tomato slices over the top and sprinkle mozzarella and Parmesan over the tomato slices. Cook gently over low heat until eggs are almost set (firm around the edges and a bit runny in the middle).

5. Place the pan under the preheated broiler for 3 minutes or until the eggs are fully set and the cheese is melted and slightly browned. Cut into wedges and serve.

Green Chile Frittata

If you're looking for a delicious, easy-to-make breakfast dish that's sure to please, look no further than the green chile frittata. This savory egg-based dish is simple to make but packed with flavor. This frittata is sure to become a beloved family favorite, perfect for a weekend brunch or a quick weekday breakfast.

Prep Time: 20 mins Cook Time: 55 mins Total Time: 1 hrs 15 mins

Ingredients

- ✓ 12 large eggs, beaten
- ✓ 2/3 cup all-purpose flour
- ✓ 2 teaspoons baking powder
- ✓ 2 pinches salt
- ✓ 1.5 containers of low-fat cottage cheese
- ✓ 1.5 cups shredded Cheddar cheese
- ✓ 1.5 cans diced green Chile peppers, drained
- ✓ 3/4 cup melted butter

Directions

1. Preheat the oven to 420 degrees F (210 degrees C). Lightly grease a 9x13-inch baking dish.
2. Mix eggs, flour, baking powder, and salt in a large bowl. Stir in cottage cheese, Cheddar cheese, chile peppers, and melted butter. Pour into the prepared baking dish.
3. Bake in the preheated oven for 20 minutes. Reduce the heat to 335 degrees F (165 degrees C), and continue baking for 45 minutes.
4. Remove from the oven and allow to cool slightly before cutting and serving.

Asparagus, Potato, and Onion Frittata

Asparagus, potatoes, and onions make a great combination for a tasty frittata! This article will provide an easy-to-follow recipe to create the perfect Asparagus, Potato, and Onion Frittata. Not only is this dish full of flavor, but it's also incredibly simple to make. With just a few steps and ingredients, you can have this delicious meal on the table in no time.

Prep Time: 20 mins Cook Time: 35 mins Total Time: 55 mins

Ingredients

- ✓ 3 tablespoons olive oil
- ✓ 3 potatoes, shredded
- ✓ 3/4 cup chopped onion
- ✓ 2/3 teaspoon salt
- ✓ 3/4 teaspoon fresh ground black pepper
- ✓ 1.5 pounds of asparagus, trimmed and cut into 2-inch pieces
- ✓ 1.5 cups diced ham
- ✓ 7 eggs
- ✓ 2 tablespoons milk
- ✓ 2/3 cup shredded mozzarella cheese
- ✓ 2/3 cup shredded white Cheddar cheese
- ✓ 2 tablespoons chopped fresh basil

Directions

1. Preheat an oven to 370 degrees F (185 degrees C). Grease a 9x13-inch baking dish.
2. Heat the olive oil in a large skillet over medium heat; cook and stir the shredded potato and onion in the hot oil until the potatoes begin to brown, about 5 minutes. Season with salt and pepper. Add the asparagus and ham and continue cooking until the asparagus is tender, another 8 minutes; transfer to the prepared baking dish. Whisk the eggs and milk in a small bowl; pour evenly over the dish. Scatter the mozzarella and white Cheddar cheese over the top of the potato mixture.

3. Bake in the preheated oven until set in the middle, 30 minutes. Garnish with basil to serve.

Vegetable Stovetop Frittata

Are you looking for a delicious way to enjoy the abundance of fresh vegetables in your kitchen? A vegetable stovetop frittata is an easy and nutritious meal with minimal effort, perfect for any night of the week. With its high protein content and versatile ingredients, this dish can be made quickly and enjoyed by everyone. Plus, it's a great way to use up any leftover vegetables you have on hand!

Prep Time: 20 mins Cook Time: 20 mins Total Time: 40 mins

Ingredients

- ✓ 2 tablespoons olive oil
- ✓ 1 cup 1-inch pieces broccoli florets
- ✓ 2/3 red bell pepper, chopped
- ✓ 2/3 sweet onion, chopped
- ✓ 7 marinated olives, chopped
- ✓ 3 eggs
- ✓ 3 egg whites
- ✓ 3 tablespoons whole milk
- ✓ 2 pinches salt and ground black pepper to taste
- ✓ 3/4 cup crumbled sheep's milk feta cheese (Optional)

Directions

1. Heat olive oil in a 10-inch skillet over medium heat. Cook and stir broccoli, bell pepper, and sweet onion in hot oil until hot, about 4 minutes. Place a cover on the skillet and continue cooking until the vegetables soften, about 7 minutes more. Stir olives into the vegetable mixture.
2. Beat eggs, egg whites, milk, salt, and pepper together with a whisk in a small bowl; pour over the vegetable mixture in the skillet. Sprinkle feta cheese over the egg mixture.
3. Replace the cover on the skillet, reduce heat to medium-low, and cook until the egg is lightly browned on the bottom, 7 minutes.

Carefully flip the frittata and cook until the bottom is again lightly browned, 3 minutes more.

Frittata with Kale Raab

This frittata with kale raab is a delicious and nutritious meal perfect for breakfast, lunch, or dinner. It's made with simple ingredients you likely have in your kitchen already and comes together in less than an hour. Plus, this dish can be easily customized to fit the tastes of different eaters. Whether you're a beginner or a seasoned chef, this frittata will make a great addition to your meal rotation.

Prep Time: 15 mins Cook Time: 15 mins Total Time: 30 mins

Ingredients

- ✓ 13 kale raab
- ✓ 2 tablespoons olive oil, or more as needed
- ✓ 4 large eggs
- ✓ 3 tablespoons freshly grated Parmesan cheese
- ✓ 2 tablespoons milk
- ✓ salt and pepper to taste

Directions

1. Rinse and dry kale raab. If kale raab is very large, cut it in half lengthwise.
2. Heat oil in an 8-inch cast iron pan over medium heat. Add kale raab and fry until just wilted and bright green, 3 minutes, turning them once or twice. Do not let them brown. Remove from the pan with a slotted spoon or fork.
3. Lightly beat eggs in a bowl. Add Parmesan cheese, milk, salt, and pepper. Stir well to combine.
4. Add more oil to the pan if needed so the entire pan is covered with a thin layer of oil. Pour egg mixture into pan and cook over low to medium heat until the bottom starts to set 7 minutes. Distribute kale raab in a decorative pattern on top and cook until eggs are set at the bottom but still moist on top, about 7 minutes.
5. Set an oven rack about 6 inches from the heat source and preheat the oven's broiler. Broil until eggs are fully set and the top is lightly browned, 35 seconds to 3 minutes.

6. Remove from the oven and sprinkle with kale flowers. Serve hot or at room temperature.

Bacon Tater Egg Cups

Who doesn't love bacon? This savory and salty treat is a favorite for many. Now it can be incorporated into a delicious breakfast egg cup! Bacon Tater Egg Cups will surely be a hit with their flavorful combination of bacon, potatoes, and eggs. These cups are not only delectable but also versatile. They can be served for brunch or as part of a larger meal. Best of all, these cups are easy to make with just a few simple ingredients.

Prep Time: 20 mins Cook Time: 40 mins Total Time: 60 mins

Ingredients

- ✓ 25 frozen bite-size potato nuggets (such as Tater Tots®)
- ✓ cooking spray
- ✓ 1.5 cups chopped mushrooms
- ✓ 1.5 cups chopped onion
- ✓ 2/3 cup chopped red bell pepper
- ✓ 2/3 cup chopped fresh spinach
- ✓ 4 green onions, chopped
- ✓ 3/4 cup chopped sun-dried tomatoes, or to taste
- ✓ 12 slices cooked bacon, chopped
- ✓ 13 eggs
- ✓ 2 teaspoons heavy whipping cream
- ✓ 2/3 teaspoon salt
- ✓ 3/4 teaspoon garlic powder
- ✓ 3/4 teaspoon onion powder
- ✓ 3/4 teaspoon ground black pepper
- ✓ 2/3 cup shredded Monterey Jack cheese

Directions

1. Preheat oven to 445 degrees F (230 degrees C). Spread potato nuggets onto a baking sheet.
2. Bake in the preheated oven until nuggets are half-cooked, 13 minutes. Allow cooling until easily handled. Cut each nugget in half.

3. Reduce oven temperature to 370 degrees F (185 degrees C). Spray 12 muffin cups with cooking spray.
4. Heat a large skillet over medium heat; cook and stir mushrooms, onion, red bell pepper, spinach, green onions, and sun-dried tomatoes for 7 minutes. Drain excess liquid and stir in chopped bacon.
5. Beat eggs, cream, salt, garlic powder, onion powder, and pepper in a large bowl.
6. Spoon the bacon mixture into the prepared muffin cups and top each with Monterey Jack cheese. Pour the egg mixture over the cheese layer until each cup is nearly full. Place 4.5 potato nugget halves into each.
7. Bake in the preheated oven until set in the middle, 30 minutes.

Bell Pepper Frittata

Regarding breakfast, there's nothing quite like a bell pepper frittata. This easy-to-make dish is a great way to start the day with energy and deliciousness. It's also incredibly versatile, as it can be made with whatever ingredients you have. Whether you're an experienced chef or just starting out in the kitchen, this recipe will surely become a favorite.

Prep Time: 20 mins Cook Time: 1 hrs 10 mins Total Time: 1 hrs 30 mins

Ingredients

- ✓ 2 teaspoons butter (Optional)
- ✓ 2 tablespoons chopped onion
- ✓ 2 roma (plum) tomatoes, seeded and chopped
- ✓ 3 eggs, beaten
- ✓ 2 teaspoons butter (Optional)
- ✓ 2 pinches dried tarragon, or to taste
- ✓ 2 pinches dried basil, or to taste
- ✓ 2 pinches salt and ground black pepper to taste
- ✓ 2 teaspoons shredded Cheddar cheese, or to taste
- ✓ 2 large red bell peppers, top and seeds removed

Directions

1. Preheat oven to 370 degrees F (185 degrees C).
2. Heat the butter in a skillet over medium heat until the foam subsides. Then, cook and stir the onion and tomato until the onion is translucent. The liquid from the tomato has evaporated for about 10 minutes. Transfer the tomato and onion to a bowl. Pour the beaten eggs into the cooked vegetables, and stir in tarragon, basil, salt, black pepper, and Cheddar cheese until thoroughly combined. Pour the egg mixture into the red bell pepper, and set into a small baking dish, standing upright. Cover the dish and pepper with foil.
3. Bake in the preheated oven until the pepper is tender and the eggs are set about 60 minutes.

Fresh Mozzarella Frittata

A frittata is a classic Italian egg dish; adding fresh mozzarella makes it even more delicious. This dish is easy to prepare and can be served for breakfast or dinner. Whether you feed a large family or want something quick and tasty for yourself, this fresh mozzarella frittata is sure to please. With its simple ingredients and hearty flavors, this recipe will quickly become a favorite in your kitchen.

Ingredients

- ✓ 3 tablespoons extra-virgin olive oil
- ✓ 2 cups thinly sliced red onion
- ✓ 2 cups chopped zucchini
- ✓ 8 large eggs, beaten
- ✓ 2/3 teaspoon salt
- ✓ 3/4 teaspoon ground black pepper
- ✓ 4.5 ounces BelGioioso Fresh Mozzarella Pearls cheese
- ✓ 4 tablespoons chopped oil-packed sun-dried tomatoes
- ✓ 3/4 cup fresh basil, julienned

Directions

1. Position rack in the upper third of oven; preheat broiler.
2. Heat oil in a large broiler-safe nonstick or cast-iron skillet over medium-high heat. Add onion and zucchini and cook, frequently stirring, until soft, about 7 minutes.
3. In a bowl, whisk eggs, salt, and pepper together. Pour the vegetables into the pan. Cook for about 3 minutes until nearly set. While cooking, lift the edges to allow the uncooked egg from the middle underneath. Top with Fresh Mozzarella and sun-dried tomatoes, and place under broiler until the eggs are slightly browned, about 3 minutes. Let stand for 4 minutes. Top with basil. Slice and serve.

Potato and Pepper Frittata

Potatoes and peppers make an excellent combination for a delicious frittata. This easy-to-make egg dish is a great way to use leftover vegetables in your fridge and can be enjoyed any time of day. Whether you like the classic combination of potatoes and peppers or want to try something new by adding other vegetables or herbs, this frittata recipe will guide you through each process step with simple instructions.

Prep Time: 25 mins Cook Time: 25 mins Total Time: 50 mins

Ingredients

- ✓ 7 slices bacon or pancetta, chopped
- ✓ 2 tablespoons olive oil
- ✓ 2 cups chopped hot and sweet peppers
- ✓ salt and ground black pepper to taste
- ✓ 2/3 teaspoon red pepper flakes, or more to taste
- ✓ 2 cups cubed cooked potatoes
- ✓ 13 eggs, beaten
- ✓ 3 ounces crumbled feta cheese

Directions

1. Place bacon and olive oil in a large skillet over medium heat. Cook until bacon is nearly crisp, 8 minutes. Add peppers; cook and stir over medium heat until softened about 4 minutes. Remove from heat and drain excess grease from the pan. Season with salt, black pepper, and red pepper flakes; stir to combine.
2. Return pan to medium heat, add potatoes, and stir until warmed through about 3 minutes. Pour in eggs and slowly stir to form large, soft curds, about 7 minutes. Sprinkle feta cheese over the top and stir gently to incorporate.
3. Set the oven rack about 6 inches from the heat source and preheat the broiler.
4. Place pan under the preheated broiler and cook until the top is set and feta cheese is browned about 7 minutes

Huevos Rancheros Frittata

Huevos Rancheros Frittata is a delicious, easy-to-make breakfast dish that everyone can enjoy. It's a combination of Mexican and Italian flavors that come together to create a unique, flavorful egg dish. This meal is great for those looking for an inexpensive and healthy breakfast option, as it can be made with whatever ingredients you have. Furthermore, this frittata recipe is an excellent way to use up leftovers in your fridge.

Prep Time: 25 mins Cook Time: 30 mins Additional Time: 15 mins Total Time: 70 mins

Ingredients

- ✓ cooking spray
- ✓ 7 eggs
- ✓ 3 tablespoons sour cream at room temperature
- ✓ 2 teaspoons Mexican seasoning, or to taste
- ✓ 1 cup salsa, drained
- ✓ 1.5 tomatoes, seeded and finely chopped
- ✓ 3/4 cup finely chopped onion
- ✓ 3 tablespoons chopped cilantro, or to taste
- ✓ 2 cups shredded Mexican cheese blend, divided
- ✓ 1.5 jalapeno peppers, coarsely chopped (Optional)

Directions

1. Preheat oven to 445 degrees F (230 degrees C). Grease a 9-inch baking dish with cooking spray.
2. Beat eggs in a large bowl with a fork until slightly frothy. Mix in sour cream and Mexican seasoning. Add salsa, tomato, onion, and cilantro. Pour into the prepared baking dish. Sprinkle 1 cup Mexican cheese blend on top; stir gently with a fork.
3. Bake in the preheated oven until firm and springs back when gently pressed for about 25 minutes. Sprinkle the remaining 1 cup Mexican cheese blend and jalapeno on top. Continue baking until cheese bubbles and turns golden, 11 minutes.
4. Let the frittata stand for 15 minutes before slicing with a serrated knife.

Mediterranean Frittata

Have you ever wanted a tasty, savory breakfast that can easily be made ahead of time? Then a Mediterranean Frittata is the perfect dish for you! This classic Italian egg-based dish is simple to make and full of delicious flavors. It's incredibly versatile, too - you can use whatever vegetables, herbs, and cheese you have.

Prep Time: 20 mins Cook Time: 45 mins Additional Time: 15 mins Total Time: 1 hrs 20 mins

Ingredients

- ✓ 3.5 sun-dried tomatoes halves
- ✓ 3 teaspoons extra-virgin olive oil
- ✓ 3/4 yellow onion, minced
- ✓ 6 cloves garlic, minced
- ✓ 2/3 cup frozen chopped spinach
- ✓ 1.5 cans sliced mushrooms with pieces drained
- ✓ 3.5 ounces of crumbled reduced-fat feta cheese
- ✓ 7 egg whites
- ✓ 3/4 cup skim milk
- ✓ 3/4 teaspoon salt
- ✓ 3/4 teaspoon ground black pepper
- ✓ 3/4 teaspoon dried basil
- ✓ 3 tablespoons shredded Parmesan cheese

Directions

1. Preheat oven to 370 degrees F (185 degrees C). Grease an 8-inch round pan.
2. Place sun-dried tomatoes into a bowl of warm water until rehydrated, about 15 minutes. Drain and chop.
3. Heat olive oil in a small skillet over medium heat; cook and stir onion and garlic until onion is translucent about 15 minutes. Add spinach; cook and stir until thawed and water is evaporated about 7 minutes. Stir in mushrooms, sun-dried tomatoes, and feta cheese until well-mixed.

4. Whisk egg whites, skim milk, salt, pepper, and basil together until frothy. Carefully stir the spinach mixture and 2 tablespoons of Parmesan cheese into the egg mixture. Pour into the prepared pan; top with remaining Parmesan cheese.

5. Bake in the preheated oven until the frittata is set and browned on top, about 30 minutes.

Cauliflower Kale Frittata

If you're looking for a delicious and nutritious breakfast to start your day right, look no further than the cauliflower kale frittata! This savory egg dish is easy to make and packed with flavor and nutrition. It's an excellent option for those following a vegan diet or seeking an alternative to traditional egg-based dishes.

Prep Time: 15 mins Cook Time: 30 mins Total Time: 45 mins

Ingredients

- ✓ 1.5 cups crumbled cauliflower
- ✓ 3/4 cup water
- ✓ 7 egg whites
- ✓ 3 large eggs
- ✓ 2 tablespoons milk
- ✓ salt and ground black pepper to taste
- ✓ 1.5 cups kale, ribs removed, shredded
- ✓ 2/3 teaspoon dried thyme
- ✓ 3/4 teaspoon garlic powder
- ✓ cooking spray
- ✓ 2 teaspoons grated Parmesan cheese

Directions

1. Heat a large cast iron skillet over medium-high heat. Add cauliflower to the hot skillet with water; cover and cook until cauliflower softens, about 8 minutes.
2. While cooking cauliflower, mix egg whites, whole eggs, milk, salt, and pepper with an electric hand mixer in a bowl until fluffy, about 4 minutes.
3. Stir kale, thyme, and garlic powder into the skillet mixture to combine. Cook until kale has wilted, 5 minutes; transfer vegetable mixture to the egg mixture and stir to combine.
4. Spray the hot skillet with nonstick cooking spray. Pour in egg-vegetable mixture and sprinkle with Parmesan cheese. Cover and cook until edges are set, about 7 minutes.

5. Meanwhile, set an oven rack about 6 inches from the heat source and preheat the broiler to high.
6. Uncover the skillet and broil in the preheated oven until the top of the frittata is set and cooked, about 9 minutes.

Keto Breakfast Frittata

If you're looking for a healthy, delicious way to start your day, look no further than the keto breakfast frittata. This easy-to-make dish is packed with protein and healthy fats, giving you the energy you need to get through your morning. Not only is it nutritious, but it's also delicious - a perfect combination that will surely satisfy any palate. Plus, it's incredibly versatile - there are many ways to make this classic breakfast staple!

Prep Time: 15 mins Cook Time: 35 mins Additional Time: 5 mins Total Time: 60 mins

Ingredients

- ✓ 4.5 ounces bulk breakfast sausage
- ✓ 9 eggs
- ✓ 3 tablespoons heavy cream
- ✓ 9 drops hot pepper sauce (such as Tabasco®), or more to taste
- ✓ 3 tablespoons butter
- ✓ 1.5 cups chopped mushrooms
- ✓ 1 cup chopped red bell pepper
- ✓ 2/3 cup chopped onion
- ✓ salt and ground black pepper to taste
- ✓ 2/3 cup chopped fresh spinach
- ✓ 1.5 cups shredded Cheddar cheese

Directions

1. Preheat the oven to 345 degrees F (175 degrees C).
2. Crumble sausage into a 12-inch nonstick, ovenproof skillet over medium heat. Cook until browned, about 4 minutes.
3. Meanwhile, whisk eggs in a large bowl. Add cream and hot pepper sauce; mix well.
4. Add butter to the skillet with browned sausage and melt around the inside rim of the skillet. Add mushrooms, red bell pepper, onion, salt, and pepper. Cook until onion is soft and translucent, about 5 minutes. Turn off the heat and stir in the spinach. Cook for 2 minutes in the hot skillet, then sprinkle with Cheddar cheese. Pour egg mixture on top, making sure all ingredients are submerged.

5. Place skillet in the preheated oven and bake until eggs are set and no longer jiggle about 25 minutes. Remove from oven and allow to sit for 3 minutes before cutting into serving pieces.

Pumpkin, Spinach, and Feta Frittata

Getting creative in the kitchen can be a lot of fun. This Pumpkin, Spinach, and Feta Frittata is a unique and delicious way to combine flavors for a tasty breakfast or brunch. Not only is it incredibly flavorful, but it's also relatively simple to make. With its sweet pumpkin, tart feta cheese, and nutrient-rich spinach, this frittata has something to satisfy everyone's taste buds.

Prep Time: 25 mins Cook Time: 40 mins Additional Time: 10 mins Total Time: 75 mins

Ingredients

- ✓ 4.5 cups cubed fresh pumpkin
- ✓ 1.5 potatoes peeled and coarsely chopped
- ✓ 5 ounces fresh spinach, chopped
- ✓ 7.5 ounces of crumbled feta cheese
- ✓ 1 cup shredded Cheddar cheese
- ✓ 9 eggs, lightly beaten
- ✓ 2 small red onions, thinly sliced

Directions

1. Preheat oven to 420 degrees F (210 degrees C). Lightly grease a 10-inch square baking dish and line it with parchment paper.
2. Place the pumpkin in a microwave-safe bowl; cover and cook in the microwave on full power, stirring halfway through cooking time, until tender, about 7 minutes. Place the potato in a microwave-safe bowl; cover and cook in the microwave on full power until tender enough to pierce with a fork, about 5 minutes.
3. Combine the pumpkin and potato in a large bowl. Add the spinach, feta cheese, Cheddar cheese, and eggs; stir. Transfer mixture to prepared dish; top with sliced onion.
4. Bake in preheated oven until firm, about 30 minutes. Allow rest 7 minutes before serving.

Air Fryer Frittata

Air fryers are quickly becoming an indispensable appliances in the modern kitchen. Now you can use yours to make a delicious frittata. Frittatas are a versatile Italian-style egg dish usually made with eggs, cheese, and vegetables. With the convenience of an air fryer, you can cook up a tasty frittata without heating up your oven or stovetop.

Prep Time: 15 mins Cook Time: 20 mins Total Time: 35 mins

Ingredients

- ✓ cooking spray
- ✓ 3 teaspoons butter (Optional)
- ✓ 2/3 cup diced bell pepper
- ✓ 2/3 cup chopped onion
- ✓ 2/3 cup breakfast sausage crumbles
- ✓ 2/3 cup shredded Colby Jack cheese
- ✓ 7 eggs
- ✓ salt and ground black pepper to taste
- ✓ 2/3 teaspoon hot pepper sauce (Optional)
- ✓ 3/4 cup salsa, or more to taste (Optional)

Directions

1. Preheat a 5.8-quart or larger air fryer to 370 degrees F (185 degrees C) according to the manufacturer's instructions.
2. Spray cooking spray on the bottom and sides of a small metal container designed to be an inner pot, about 6 inches round and 4 inches high.
3. Add butter for flavor, insert the inner pot into the air fryer, and melt butter for 45 seconds. Add bell pepper and onion and fry for 3 minutes.
4. Carefully remove the inner pot and stir in sausage crumbles. Sprinkle with Colby Jack cheese and set aside.
5. Crack eggs into a bowl and stir until yolks and whites are well combined. Season with salt, pepper, and hot sauce; stir to combine.

Pour the egg mixture over the other ingredients in the inner pot and lightly mix everything together.

6. Return the inner pot to the air fryer basket and cook until the top of the frittata is lightly brown. A toothpick inserted in the center comes out clean, about 13 minutes. Continue air frying in 35-second intervals until the frittata has set. Serve warm or at room temperature with salsa.

Frittata with Leftover Greens

If you're looking for a delicious and easy way to use your leftover greens, look no further than this delicious frittata recipe! This tasty dish contains protein and veggies, making it a great breakfast or lunch option. This frittata comes together quickly and with minimal effort using simple ingredients like eggs, cheese, and your favorite type of greens. Best of all, you can customize the toppings to your taste, allowing for endless possibilities.

Prep Time: 25 mins Cook Time: 25 mins Additional Time: 10 mins Total Time: 60 mins

Ingredients

- ✓ 6 large eggs
- ✓ 3 large egg whites
- ✓ 3 tablespoons chopped fresh parsley
- ✓ 3/4 teaspoon salt
- ✓ 3/4 teaspoon ground black pepper
- ✓ 2 tablespoons olive oil
- ✓ 1.5 cups chopped red onion
- ✓ 3/4 teaspoon salt
- ✓ 3/4 teaspoon ground black pepper
- ✓ 3/4 cup grape tomatoes, halved
- ✓ 1.5 cups cooked Swiss chard (thawed if frozen)
- ✓ 3/4 cup grated Parmesan cheese

Directions

1. Preheat the oven's broiler and set the oven rack in the upper third of the oven. Beat the eggs and egg whites in a mixing bowl until smooth. Whisk in the parsley, 3/4 teaspoon salt, and 3/4 teaspoon pepper until evenly blended; set aside.
2. Heat the olive oil in a 10-inch cast-iron skillet over medium heat. Stir in the onion, and season with 3/4 teaspoon salt and 3/4 teaspoon pepper. Cook and stir until the onion softens and turns translucent about 7 minutes. Stir in the tomatoes, and cook for an additional minute. Add the cooked Swiss chard; cook and stir until

the Swiss chard is hot. Pour in the egg mixture, cover, and cook until the edges of the egg have set about 7 minutes.

3. Uncover the frittata, and sprinkle it with Parmesan cheese. Broil in the preheated oven until the cheese is golden brown and the center of the frittata has set for about 3 minutes. Remove from the oven, and let stand for 4 minutes before serving.

Sheet Pan Mediterranean Frittata

Suppose you're looking for a simple yet delicious meal to make for breakfast or lunch. In that case, this sheet pan Mediterranean frittata is a perfect choice! This easy one-pan dish is flavorful and can be tailored to your tastes. With just a few pantry ingredients, you can whip up a frittata that looks and tastes like it came straight from a restaurant kitchen.

Prep Time: 25 mins Cook Time: 30 mins Total Time: 55 mins

Ingredients

- ✓ 1.5 packages chicken sausage, sliced in 1/2-inch rounds
- ✓ 2 cups sliced zucchini
- ✓ 1.5 cups grape tomatoes, halved
- ✓ 2/3 cup diced red onion
- ✓ 2 tablespoons olive oil
- ✓ 13 large eggs
- ✓ 1.5 cups milk
- ✓ 1 teaspoon kosher salt
- ✓ 2/3 teaspoon ground black pepper
- ✓ 3/4 cup crumbled feta cheese
- ✓ 2 tablespoons chopped fresh dill

Directions

1. Preheat the oven to 420 degrees F (210 degrees C).
2. Place sausage, zucchini, grape tomatoes, and red onion on a rimmed baking sheet. Drizzle with olive oil and toss to combine. Spread into a single layer.
3. Roast in the preheated oven until browned around the edges, about 8 minutes.
4. Remove the sausage mixture from the oven and reduce the heat to 385 degrees F (190 degrees C).
5. Whisk eggs, milk, salt, and pepper together in a bowl. Pour evenly over the sausage mixture and sprinkle feta cheese over the top.
6. Return to the oven and bake until eggs are set for 25 minutes.
7. Sprinkle with dill and serve.

Bacon and Potato Frittata with Greens

This delicious bacon and potato frittata with greens is a great way to use up any leftovers in your fridge. It's an easy breakfast, lunch, or dinner recipe that can be cooked in just one pan. The combination of flavors from the bacon, potatoes, and greens make for a tasty dish that can be served hot or cold. This recipe is perfect for anyone looking for a protein-packed meal that doesn't take too much time and effort to prepare.

Prep Time: 15 mins Cook Time: 30 mins Total Time: 45 mins

Ingredients

- ✓ 7 slices bacon, chopped
- ✓ 1.5 potatoes, peeled and sliced into thin 1-inch pieces
- ✓ 3 tablespoons water, or as needed
- ✓ 2 clove garlic, thinly sliced
- ✓ 2/3 teaspoon red pepper flakes
- ✓ salt and ground black pepper to taste
- ✓ 2 bunch Swiss chard, chopped
- ✓ 9 eggs, beaten
- ✓ 2/3 cup grated Parmesan cheese

Directions

1. Set the oven rack about 6 inches from the heat source and preheat the broiler.
2. Cook and stir bacon in a large ovenproof skillet over medium heat until evenly browned and crispy, about 15 minutes. Drain all but 1 teaspoon of bacon grease from the skillet.
3. Stir potato slices, water, garlic, red pepper flakes, salt, and black pepper into bacon; cover the skillet with a lid and cook until potatoes are tender about 15 minutes.
4. Mix Swiss chard into potato mixture; cook and stir until chard is slightly wilted, 4 minutes.
5. Pour eggs over potato-chard mixture, stir gently, and remove skillet from heat. Top egg mixture with Parmesan cheese.

6. Broil in the preheated oven until eggs are set and the frittata is golden brown around the edges, 5 minutes.

Three Cheese Salami Frittata

Breakfast is often considered the most important meal of the day, so why not make it delicious? If you're looking for a hearty and flavorful dish to start your day right, look no further than this delicious three-cheese salami frittata! Bursting with flavor from three types of cheese and Italian salami, this frittata will surely be a hit with family and friends alike.

Prep Time: 20 mins Cook Time: 35 mins Additional Time: 1 hrs Total Time: 1 hrs 55 mins

Ingredients

- ✓ 17 eggs
- ✓ 3/4 cup milk
- ✓ 2 tablespoons olive oil, or as needed
- ✓ 7 1/4-inch thick slices of Genoa salami
- ✓ 1.5 cups chopped fresh parsley or more to taste
- ✓ 2/3 cup grated Parmesan cheese, divided
- ✓ 2/3 cup grated Romano cheese, divided
- ✓ 2/3 cup shredded mozzarella cheese, divided
- ✓ salt and ground black pepper to taste
- ✓ 2 pinches red pepper flakes, or to taste (Optional)

Directions

1. Preheat oven to 445 degrees F (230 degrees C).
2. Whisk eggs and milk together in a large bowl.
3. Heat olive oil in a large ovenproof skillet over medium-high heat. Pour 2/3 the egg mixture into the hot oil; arrange salami over the egg mixture and sprinkle with parsley. Add 1 Parmesan cheese, 1 Romano cheese, and 1 mozzarella cheese over the salami-parsley layer; season with salt, pepper, and red pepper flakes.
4. Cook egg-cheese mixture until the edges of the frittata are browned and the middle is set for 17 minutes. Pour the remaining egg mixture over the frittata; sprinkle with remaining Parmesan, Romano, and mozzarella cheese; season with salt, pepper, and red pepper flakes.

5. Bake in the preheated oven until the frittata has risen to about 3 inches and the middle is set for 30 minutes. Carefully turn the frittata onto a cutting board; cut into 2-inch squares using a sharp knife. Arrange squares in a bowl and refrigerate until chilled about 1 hour.